Summary

of the

National

Directory

for Catechesis

COMMITTEE ON CATECHESIS
United States Conference of
Catholic Bishops

United States Conference of Catholic Bishops
Washington, D.C.

The *Summary of the "National Directory for Catechesis"* was developed as a resource by the Committee on Catechesis of the United States Conference of Catholic Bishops (USCCB). It was reviewed by the Committee on Catechesis, was approved by the committee chairman, Archbishop Daniel M. Buechlein, OSB, and has been authorized for publication by the undersigned.

Msgr. William P. Fay
General Secretary, USCCB

Cover: *Christ Enthroned between the Virgin and St. Mark*, second half thirteenth century, Byzantine mosaic. S. Marco (nave, west wall above main doors), Venice, Italy. Copyright Cameraphoto/Art Resource, NY.

First Printing, May 2005
Second Printing, June 2005

ISBN 1-57455-696-7

Contents

Introduction

TEXTUAL NOTE: This publication is a faithful summary of each chapter of the *National Directory for Catechesis*. It is designed to provide a brief survey of the text's content, not to replace the text itself, where principles and guidelines for catechetical instruction are presented in full.

The Second Vatican Council called for the renewal of catechesis. This call resulted in the promulgation of many significant universal Church documents: the *General Catechetical Directory* (1971), *Rite of Christian Initiation of Adults* (1972), Pope Paul VI's apostolic exhortation *On Evangelization in the Modern World* (1975), and Pope John Paul II's *On Catechesis in Our Time* (1979). Under the leadership of Pope John Paul II, who has zealously contributed to the renewal of catechesis in the contemporary Church, the *Catechism of the Catholic Church* (1992) and the *General Directory for Catechesis* (1997) together represent a synthesis of catechetical ministry for the universal church.

The documents intended for the whole Church have served as the inspiration and foundation for our own national catechetical directories: *Sharing the Light of Faith* (1979) and the new *National Directory for Catechesis* (2005), both of which are official documents of the United States Conference of Catholic Bishops. The *National Directory for Catechesis*, reviewed and approved by the Congregation for the Clergy in the Holy See, provides fundamental theological and pastoral principles, drawn from the Church's Magisterium, for the pastoral activity of catechesis in parishes and dioceses within the United States. The *National Directory for Catechesis* is intended primarily for those who have responsibility for catechesis in dioceses, parishes, and schools; but all those who participate in the Church's mission to proclaim the Gospel will find it useful. The *National Directory for Catechesis* is also a fundamental reference for authors, editors, and publishers of catechetical texts and other catechetical resources. The guidelines in the *National Directory for Catechesis*, which are aimed at the continued renewal of catechesis in the United States, set forth the nature, purpose, aims, tasks, basic content, and methodologies of catechesis.

Although some members of the Church are called to more specific catechetical roles, fostering growth in faith is the responsibility of the entire Christian community. The *National Directory for Catechesis* will be a source of hope and encouragement to all who participate, directly and indirectly, in catechetical ministry—deepening their reliance upon God, and helping them recognize how God, Father, Son, and Holy Spirit, works in and through them to bring the message of salvation to all.

1

Proclaiming the Gospel in the United States

Catechesis necessarily occurs within a social and cultural context. Thus, catechists must consider the Christian message in relation to the particular circumstances in which they announce it.

The Holy Spirit is the primary agent of evangelization, who makes possible the encounter between the Word of God and the many diverse languages and cultures throughout the world. In this context, the first chapter of the *National Directory for Catechesis* describes the cultural and religious factors that currently affect catechesis in the United States, discussed under four main headings: (1) general characteristics of U.S. culture, (2) diversity in U.S. culture, (3) a profile of Catholics in the United States, and (4) family and home in the United States.

General Characteristics of U.S. Culture

U.S. culture is marked, first and foremost, by great emphasis on *freedom*. This God-given right to freedom is in itself a positive value, underlying the pluralism and diversity for which the United States is known. However, many distortions of genuine freedom exist in our nation: most significantly, the exaggerated emphasis on an individual's freedom and rights. Such a distorted view of freedom can result in moral relativism and privatization of religion.

A second characteristic of U.S. culture is the value it places on *religious freedom*. The principle of separation of church and state holds that government must not establish a single religion as the religion of the state or prefer one religion over another. The government must also protect the free exercise of religion in all states. This principle has enabled people of different faiths to find a home in America. However, the principle of religious freedom has also been construed as calling for the complete separation of religion from public life.

Economic freedom is a third quality important in U.S. culture. The principles of individual responsibility, equal opportunity, and the free enterprise system govern American economic freedom. While most agree that individuals should enjoy equal access to economic and social opportunities, a wide gap exists between rich and poor. Because of this gap, the Catholic faith upholds the need to judge economic decisions or institutions by the extent to which they protect human dignity and allow participation of all.

Pragmatism, a focus on practical rather than intellectual knowledge, is a fourth trait permeating U.S. culture. While a pragmatic orientation has positive aspects, pragmatism can also encourage a utilitarian attitude—that is, the idea that something has value only to the degree that it is concretely useful.

Developments in *science and technology* represent both blessing and challenge. Many of these developments promote the good of the whole human community. However, they also create the ability to produce unconscionable evil. The rapidity of these scientific advances often leads to situations in which the means to do something is discovered before the ramifications are given adequate consideration. The moral good or evil of developments cannot simply be based on some promised benefit of a particular technological development—the intrinsic nature of the means and the implications for the well-being of the human person and human community must also be assessed.

A worldwide force affecting U.S. culture is rapid *globalization*. In positive ways, globalization has led to higher standards of living for many. But a negative effect of globalization has been an increase in the already wide gap between rich and poor peoples and nations. The Gospel calls all to global responsibility and solidarity, which includes the protection of the poor and vulnerable in the United States and around the world. U.S. Catholics have a special responsibility to work toward solidarity, in part because the United States, more than any other nation, bears great responsibility for cultural and economic globalization.

Finally, *mobility* in the United States continues to shape its culture. Immigration, transportation, and communications technology have resulted in community life that is based more on affinity than on geographic or neighborhood contexts. This has a profound effect on parish life and catechesis. For example, many Catholics look for parishes and religious education programs where they can enjoy a strong sense of community—and do not automatically join those communities and programs that are geographically closest.

Diversity in U.S. Culture

The United States is marked by great cultural and religious diversity, representing nearly all ethnicities and religious traditions.

Diversity Within the Catholic Church

Catholics in the United States, representing 23 percent of the general population,[1] are a diverse mixture of races, ethnicities, and cultures. This cultural pluralism within the Church is a positive value, and the distinctive identities of each culture should be preserved even while unity of faith is promoted.

Many Eastern Catholic Churches are also active in the United States. Together, in communion with the pope, these Churches are a visible sign of the unity of the Church of Christ, and the resulting diversity of expression united in the one faith enriches the Church.

Regional Diversity

Each region of the United States has particular geography and demographics, and each also comprises various religious groups. The Northeast is dominated by mainline Protestant traditions and is also home to large numbers of Catholics; it is more secularized and urbanized than the Midwest and the South. In the South, evangelical Protestant faiths and other religious bodies play a special role in the culture. The Midwest combines aspects of the more secular Northeast and the more socially conservative and evangelical Protestant South. The West has the fewest inhabitants who indicate any affiliation with organized religion; in the Pacific Northwest in particular, anti-Catholicism is a reality.[2]

Profile of Catholics in the United States

The current population of Catholics in the United States is 62 million and growing, and the number of dioceses and eparchies has also grown. Parish life has generally increased in scale and complexity. Twenty-two percent of parishes celebrate Mass in languages other than English at least once a month, with Spanish being the second language in the vast majority of these parishes.[3]

At the same time, the number of parishes without full-time pastors has increased. The number of priests, both diocesan and religious, has not kept pace with the growth of the Catholic population. The number of Catholic parishes with schools has decreased, even as the number of young Catholics participating in parish-based religious education programs has grown.

In addition, the numbers of women and men religious have declined by half since the 1960s, and their average age is more than sixty-three years.

Meanwhile, lay ministers have greatly increased in number. Some have pursued professional training and serve as parish and diocesan leaders in catechesis, Liturgy, and pastoral ministry. Many more serve as catechists, RCIA team members, liturgical ministers, youth ministers, social justice advocates, parish council and committee members, and ecumenical representatives.

Family and Home in the United States

Family and home life in the United States show positive trends, and policy makers have increasingly acknowledged the need to address family concerns in public policy. Yet negative elements also plague marriage and family life in the United States, and for Catholics in particular: high divorce rates, a high rate of cohabitation among those who come for marriage preparation, the decline of traditional nuclear families, and the increase of single-parent households.

Four trends underlie these social changes. First, respect for human life is challenged by the acceptance of abortion, the move toward physician-assisted suicide, and a pro-contraceptive mentality. Second, the essential bond between husband and wife is challenged by individualism. Third, the natural authority of parents over children is challenged by a distorted sense of self-sufficiency and autonomy. Finally, the transmission of traditional values within the family is challenged by popular culture and by the mobility of migrant families.

The Catholic Church offers an alternative to these forces by upholding its vision of marriage and family, reminding all of the importance of the family as the domestic church, and looking to the Trinity as the model of family life.

Notes

1   See Barry Kosim, Egon Mayer, and Ariela Keysar, *American Religious Identification Survey* (New York: Graduate Center of the City of New York, 2001), 12.

2   See Frank Hobbs and Nicole Stoops, *Demographic Trends in the Twentieth Century* (Washington, DC: U.S. Census Bureau, 2002); Edwin S. Gaustad and Philip L. Barlow, *The New Historical Atlas of Religion in America* (Oxford: Oxford University Press, 2001).

3   See *The Official Catholic Directory* (New Providence, NJ: P. J. Kenedy & Sons, 2002); Center for Applied Research in the Apostolate (CARA), *Special Report: National Parish Inventory* (NPI) (Washington, DC: CARA, 2000).

2

Catechesis Within the Church's Mission of Evangelization

The Church exists to evangelize. Evangelization expresses the Church's identity and completes the mission entrusted to her by her founder, Jesus Christ. Catechesis is a significant moment in the process of evangelization. Through comprehensive, systematic instruction and initiation into the life of the community through the Liturgy, sacraments, and service, catechesis deepens and strengthens the believer as a member of the Body of Christ, the Church.

Christ calls all members of the Church to proclaim Christ to every generation. Christians evangelize by professing faith in Christ, celebrating the Christian mysteries in the Liturgy, praying, and embracing the Christian way of life.

Catechesis is an important moment in the evangelizing mission of the Church. Catechesis echoes the word of God contained in Revelation, transmitted through Scripture and Tradition, and faithfully preserved in the teaching authority of the Church.

Revelation

Revelation is the act by which God manifests himself personally to us in order to share his divine life and to bring us into communion with him as the Father, Son, and Holy Spirit. In this way, God fulfills his plan of love for the salvation of the world and enables us, through the gift of faith, to respond to his invitation to know, love, and serve him.

God first revealed himself through creation, which he sustains and guides towards its perfect fulfillment. History also discloses God's saving plan, particularly in the covenants God made with Israel when he formed them as a people. To fulfill the covenant with David, God promised to send a Messiah and establish his kingdom forever. Revelation reached perfect fulfillment when the Word became flesh in Mary's womb and dwelt among us. Jesus Christ completed and perfected Revelation through his words, deeds, signs, and wonders and, above all, by his death and Resurrection and the sending of the Holy Spirit to remain with his disciples forever.

God's Revelation, contained in Scripture and Tradition—commonly known as the "deposit of faith"—remains living and active in the Church today, safeguarded by the Magisterium.

Faith is a gift to us from God. It has two dimensions: the faith *by which* one believes and the faith *which* one believes. *By* faith, one personally adheres to God; *through* faith, one freely assents to the truth that God reveals and transmits through the Catholic Church.

Evangelization and the Ministry of the Word

All members of the Church are called to engage actively in a *new evangelization* of the world. Directed to members of the Catholic Church seeking to revitalize their faith and sacramental worship, the new evangelization entails motivating them toward permanently engaging in catechesis; toward integrating a truly Christian spirituality into the personal, political, economic, and social aspects of life; and toward acting in favor of social justice. The new evangelization is also directed to every member of the human family and to every dimension of contemporary culture: aiming to convert to Christ those who have not previously heard or understood the Gospel, moving them to explicitly confess faith in Jesus Christ and to open themselves to transformation in Christ.

Evangelization as a ministry of the Word is realized in four stages: (1) the proclamation of Christ to non-believers and the indifferent; (2) initial catechesis for new believers; (3) continuing catechesis to deepen and mature the faith of believers; and (4) pastoral ministry to those committed to Christ.

1. *Pre-evangelization*, the initial stage, ordinarily builds on the basic human needs of those to be evangelized: food, shelter, love, security, and acceptance. Then, the Word is announced in a way the hearers can understand: to members of other religious traditions, the reli-

giously indifferent, non-believers, Christian children, Christians with minimal or deficient catechesis, and non-practicing Christians.

2. The next stage, *initiatory catechesis*, introduces catechumens, children, and those with minimal knowledge of the faith into the life of the Christian community. Through systematic instruction, prayer, initiation into sacramental life and worship, and involvement in pastoral activities of the local church, initiatory catechesis nurtures a new way of life in Christ.

3. Next, the aim of *post-baptismal catechesis* (mystagogy) is to extend and fortify the believers' relationship to Christ and the Church. Through reflection, instruction, and prayer, Christians are led to a deeper understanding of and active participation in liturgical worship and a life of charity and justice.

4. *Ongoing catechesis* deepens a believer's knowledge of Christ and the Church and helps to integrate the truths of the faith into all spheres of life: individual, family, social, economic, and political.

This catechesis can take place in a liturgical or educational setting. *Liturgical catechesis* aims to enrich and expand the meaning and impact of the sacraments in the lives of the individual and the Church. Reflection upon sacramental signs, symbols, and rituals deepens and enhances the celebration of the Liturgy, especially the Eucharist. *Theological catechesis* systematically explores and investigates the truths of the faith in dialogue with philosophy and the social sciences. It aims to make the proclamation of the Gospel meaningful to contemporary men and women and to motivate ongoing conversion to a Christian way of life.

The context for evangelization in the United States is rich and diverse. Creative methods, consistent efforts, and flexible catechetical programs are required to address negative aspects of cultural pluralism, such as moral relativism, religious indifference, alienation from institutional religion, or marginal association with the Church. The contemporary situation in our nation demands ongoing catechesis for all members of the Church, to ensure continuing conversion to a Christian way of life so that we may live by values compatible with the Gospel and reject those contrary to it.

Source and Sources of Catechesis

The source of catechesis is the Word of God revealed by Jesus Christ. All catechesis draws its content from this living source, transmitted in Scripture and

Tradition. Together, they make the revelation of Christ present, active, and fruitful in the Church.

Other sources of catechesis include liturgical worship, reflection on the word of God and the lives of the saints, prayer and actions promoting social justice, the study of theology, and the daily witness of an authentic Christian life.

Nature and Purpose of Catechesis

The aim of catechesis is to lead believers to a deeper knowledge and love of Christ and the Church and a firm commitment to follow him. Jesus Christ is at the heart of all catechesis. It is in communion with Jesus that all believers share in the mystery of the Holy Trinity—the Father, the Son, and the Holy Spirit.

Catechesis is an action of the Church and is intimately bound with the whole of the Church's life. Catechesis shapes the initial proclamation of the Gospel. It prepares for the celebration of the sacraments, facilitates integration into the ecclesial community, urges apostolic activity and missionary witness, instills a zeal for the unity of Christians, and prepares one for the ecumenical understanding and mission of the Church. The Church is the origin, locus, and goal of catechesis.

The Tasks of Catechesis

Jesus formed his disciples into a community of faith. He instructed them, prayed with them, showed them how to live, and entrusted to them the mysteries of the Kingdom of heaven. After his death and Resurrection, he sent them the Holy Spirit and commissioned them to go out and teach all nations. The fundamental task of catechesis is, therefore, to form disciples of Christ and to send them forth in mission. Following the example of Jesus the Teacher, catechesis encompasses six diverse yet interlocking tasks, as described by the *General Directory for Catechesis*:

1. Catechesis promotes knowledge of the faith.
2. Catechesis promotes meaningful participation in liturgical worship and the sacramental life of the Church.
3. Catechesis integrates moral formation into a Christian way of life.
4. Catechesis teaches Christians how to pray with Christ, in Christ, and in communion with the Church.
5. Catechesis initiates the Christian into the life of the local church community and fosters active participation in the mission of the Church.

6. Catechesis promotes a missionary spirit that prepares Christians to witness to Christ in society.

These six tasks of catechesis constitute a unified whole. While each task realizes the goal of catechesis, all of the tasks are interdependent. For catechesis to be effective, no task should be separated from the rest.

Inculturation of the Gospel Message

God's Word became flesh in Jesus Christ, a particular man born into a specific time and culture. The Incarnation of the Son of God is the divine model for inculturation and evangelization.

Every culture has the potential to welcome the gospel message proclaimed by the Church through the ages. To be effective, evangelization requires the inculturation of the gospel message. Inculturation is an interactive process that listens for echoes of the word of God in a particular culture and discerns values and practices compatible with the Gospel, purifying those that are incompatible and rejecting anything hostile to the Gospel.

In the multicultural, pluralistic social context of the United States, effective catechesis is *inculturated* catechesis, in which catechetical activity seeks to

- Discover the seeds of the Gospel present in a culture
- Respect the culture of those to whom the Gospel is addressed
- Appreciate that the gospel message transcends the limitations of human culture
- Proclaim the transforming good the Gospel can bring about in every culture
- Promote a new enthusiasm for the Gospel
- Adopt linguistic and cultural expressions that foster the transmission and reception of the gospel message
- Express coherently and convincingly the content of the faith without compromise

The catechist performs a vital role in this process. By interpreting the gospel message faithfully and communicating it understandably in the idiom of the local culture, the catechist enhances the reception of the mysteries of Christ entrusted to the Church.

3

This Is Our Faith; This Is the Faith of the Church

The content of faith is the heritage of the whole Church.
It is the privilege and responsibility of the entire people of
God to preserve the memory of Christ's words and actions and
to hand on the content of this faith to future generations.

The faith that we have received has come down to us from the Apostles. In handing on the faith that Jesus entrusted to them, the Apostles and their successors made use of short summaries or creeds that synthesized the Christian faith and were intended for catechesis, especially for candidates for Baptism. The *Catechism of the Catholic Church* is a catechesis of the Creed. Chapter 3 in the *National Directory for Catechesis* offers an introduction to the Catechism and its use in catechetical ministry.

The Symphony of the Faith

Sacred Scripture, the *Catechism of the Catholic Church*, the *General Directory for Catechesis*, and the *National Directory for Catechesis* are distinct yet harmonious instruments for the Church's catechetical ministry.

In every age of the Church, the study of Sacred Scripture has been the cornerstone of catechesis. Frequent, direct use should be made of the biblical texts themselves, and the Gospels should be presented so as to foster a relationship with Christ. The *Catechism of the Catholic Church* is a statement of the Church's faith and of Catholic doctrine, attested to or illumined by Sacred Scripture, Apostolic Tradition, and the Church's Magisterium. It is a sure and reliable reference for teaching the faith. The *Catechism* is structured around four fundamental dimensions of the Christian life: the profession of faith, the celebration of the Liturgy, Christian moral life, and prayer.

Criteria for Authentic Presentation of the Christian Message

The word of God found in Sacred Scripture and Sacred Tradition is the single source for handing on the Christian message. The presentation of the Christian message centers on the person of Jesus Christ. Every aspect of catechesis promotes following Jesus Christ. The Gospels are central to the catechetical message. They are the word of God, written by human authors inspired by the Holy Spirit.

Always Trinitarian, catechesis emphasizes the Trinity as the central mystery of Christian life. God as revealed by Jesus, the Incarnate Word, is Father, Son, and Holy Spirit. All Revelation has a Trinitarian character, and the goal of catechesis is to lead all to share in the Trinitarian communion.

Catechesis must proclaim the Good News of salvation in Jesus Christ. This salvation includes a message of liberation: liberation from all forms of sin, both personal and social. Through catechesis we come to understand that Christ inaugurated the Kingdom of God—of which the Church is the seed, the beginning. In and through the Church, we can experience aspects of the Kingdom here on earth and receive a foretaste of the eternal Kingdom of heaven.

Because the faith that is handed on is the faith of the Church, catechesis is always an ecclesial endeavor. The faith of the Church has come to us from Christ through the Apostles, recorded in the Scriptures, celebrated in the Liturgy, and manifested both in the teachings of the Magisterium and in the witness of faithful women and men through the ages. Catechesis originates in the Church's confession of faith and leads to the believer's profession of faith.

The ecclesial character of the Christian message reflects its historic nature and the Church's role in carrying on the Lord's mission. Jesus Christ is a historical figure who preached the Good News of the coming of the Reign of God in time. He established the Church to continue both his presence and his mission in every generation. This Church continues, in word and sacrament, to make present Christ in a way that enables his wisdom and teaching to be applied to the circumstances of our day and to interpret present events of human history.

The inculturation of the Gospel is a key criterion for the pastoral presentation of the Christian message. Since the ecclesial community is the principal setting for inculturation, the parish must prepare catechists in their native language and cultural situation; use culturally appropriate catechetical methods, tools, texts, and resources; foster catechetical leadership that reflects the cultural diversity; and attend to the popular devotions and feasts common to the various cultural groups within the parish.

Catechesis must also recognize and teach the hierarchical character of the Christian message. The mystery of the Most Holy Trinity is the central mystery of Christian faith and life and is therefore the most fundamental and essential of all teaching. While all the truths of faith form an organic or harmonious unity, other truths are organized around these fundamental truths: the Trinity, the Incarnation, the presence and work of the Holy Spirit, and the mystery of the Church as the Body of Christ.

The final criterion for the presentation of the Christian message is that it should foster a common language of faith so that the faith may be proclaimed, celebrated, lived, and prayed in words familiar to all the faithful. The biblical language and the formulas of faith are important because of the realities they express and the identity they foster. The contemporary relevance of traditional formulas should be explained in language suited to the people and culture being addressed.

4

Divine and Human Methodology

The transmission of the gospel message continues to be a
work of the Trinity. By God's grace, some people are
called to proclaim the Gospel as catechists. Whatever
human methods these catechists employ must be based on
the model of God's own methodology—the Father's
self-revelation in Jesus Christ and through the Holy Spirit.

Always a concern, methodology entails attention not only to the organization of content but also to age and ability and to the language and culture of the group being catechized. The paradigm for contemporary methodology derives from the pedagogy of God, which engages persons and communities in light of their circumstances and their capacity to accept and interpret Revelation, God's self-communication in Jesus through the Spirit.

God's Own Methodology

Through God's self-disclosure of the loving communion of Father, Son, and Holy Spirit, he makes known the mystery of his divine plan and its ultimate purpose—the salvation of the human person. This plan is realized gradually through God's actions and words. The way God has revealed himself to us serves as a source and model for all pedagogy of faith.

The Pedagogy of God

Since God is one God in three Divine Persons, the work of Revelation and salvation is the work of the whole Trinity. But Tradition atttributes primary agency for certain activities to each of the three Persons in accordance with their inner relation to one another.

God the Father

Through the mystery of the Incarnation, Jesus revealed God as his Father and as the Creator of all that exists. God the Father has revealed himself in other ways to people of faith in generation after generation—ways that included a covenant with his people and the Law given to Moses to help God's people live lives of faithfulness. God the Father has acted in human history in many ways and is made manifest most fully in his Son, Jesus.

Jesus Christ

As the Word of God made flesh, Jesus Christ is the sacrament of God and the preeminent model for the communication of faith and the formation of believers. The way Jesus related to his disciples as well as to the crowds whom he addressed reveals God's own methodology as the model for all catechetical methods. Jesus often began with an experience familiar to his listeners, questioned their assumptions, and finally challenged them to make a decision. His methodology was multidimensional and included words, signs, and the wonders that he worked.

The Holy Spirit

The action of the Holy Spirit in the Church continues the pedagogy of God. With Christ, the Holy Spirit animates the Church and directs her mission. The Holy Spirit makes new life in Christ possible by manifesting the Risen Lord to believers. He also opens the minds of believers to an understanding of Jesus' death and Resurrection so that they may accept the Paschal Mystery as the paradigm of their own lives.

The Church

Under the guidance of the Holy Spirit, the Church continues to catechize her members in a way that reflects and relies upon God's own methodology.

Catechesis and Divine Methodology

Catechesis as communication of divine Revelation conveys God's loving plan of salvation in the person of Jesus Christ. Building on God's own methodology, genuine catechesis

- Emphasizes God's loving initiative and the person's free response
- Accepts the progressive nature of Revelation, the transcendent and mysterious nature of the word of God, and the word's adaptation to different persons and cultures
- Recognizes the centrality of Jesus Christ
- Values the community experience of faith
- Is rooted in interpersonal relations and employs the process of dialogue
- Utilizes signs that link words and deeds, teaching and experience, and especially visible signs that express and make present the invisible reality of God's presence
- Draws from the Holy Spirit its power of truth and a commitment to bear witness to the truth

Elements of Human Methodology

The communication of faith in catechesis is, first, an event of grace under the action of the Holy Spirit, realized in the encounter of the word of God with the experience of the person. In handing on the faith, the Church does not rely on any single method. Many circumstances have to be considered, including the age and ability of the learner. Whatever the method, there should be interaction and harmony—and no opposition—between the content of faith and the method.

Catechetical methods use two basic approaches: inductive and deductive. Inductive methods begin with the experience of the learner and lead to divine truth. Deductive methods begin with the truths of faith and apply them to the concrete experience of the person. Distinct yet complementary methods for communicating the faith, both are legitimate approaches when properly applied. That is, the deductive method has full value only when the inductive method is properly utilized.

Learning takes place in many ways:

- *Human experience*, a constitutive element in catechesis, provides a starting point that must be linked to the revealed word of God in order to help people explore, interpret, and judge their basic experiences in the light of the Gospel. Human experience provides the sensible signs that lead the person by the grace of the Holy Spirit to understand the truths of the faith and the profound questions in life.
- *Learning by discipleship* is an integral element in catechesis because Christian discipleship means following Jesus Christ in one's own time, place, and circumstance.

- The witness of the *Christian community* is an important element in catechetical methodology. The effectiveness of catechesis will depend upon the vitality of the parish and the extent to which it is a clear, living, and authentic sacrament of Christ. Catechesis is the responsibility of every member of the Church.

- The *Christian family and home* ordinarily provide the most formative environment for growth in faith. It is within the Christian family that members are awakened to the presence of God and learn to pray and to form their consciences in light of the teachings of Christ and of the Church. Children learn by the selfless witness of their parents and other family members.

- The *witness of the catechist*, under the guidance of the Holy Spirit, powerfully influences those being catechized through faithful proclamation of the Gospel and the example of the catechist's life. They must firmly believe in the Gospel and its power to transform as well as live the Gospel in their own lives.

- *Learning by heart*, or memorization, is a constitutive aspect of the pedagogy of faith because it fosters a common language of faith and an identity among all the faithful. Basic prayers, creeds, key biblical themes, important figures of faith, and aspects of worship and the Christian life are memorized in order to encourage the individual to participate in what is being taught and to relate it to the whole of the Christian life. Learning by heart should continue to have a special place in catechesis today.

- *Learning by Christian living* is an essential component of catechetical methodology. Generally, the faithful can learn as they respond to God's initiative through praying, celebrating the Liturgy and sacraments, living the Christian life, fostering works of charity and of justice, addressing injustices that exist in the systemic and institutional organization of society, and promoting virtues such as liberty, solidarity, justice, peace, and protection of the environment.

- *Learning by apprenticeship* links an experienced Christian believer or mentor with one who seeks a deeper relationship with Christ and the Church. An example of learning by apprenticeship is the relationship that often develops between a catechist and a catechumen. The aim is to promote an authentic following of Christ based on the acceptance of one's baptismal responsibilities, the internalization of the word of God, and transformation to life in Christ.

Means of Communication

Much of what we know and think about today is conditioned by the various means of mass communication. For this reason, the effective use of media is essential for evangelization and catechesis. All media should be used to proclaim the gospel message. Catechists must seriously commit to learning how to use these means of communication in order to bring people to Christ. However, they must also develop a critical ability to recognize the ways in which the media promote messages contrary to gospel values.

Catechesis in a Worshiping Community

In the Liturgy, the Church both expresses faith and, through the grace of God, deepens that faith. Gathered to worship the Father in Christ and through the Holy Spirit, the Church becomes more aware of her mission to the world.

Faith and worship are closely related: faith gathers the community for worship, and worship renews the faith of the community. In the Liturgy, the official public worship of the Church, the Church celebrates what she professes and lives: above all, the Paschal Mystery by which Christ accomplished the work of our salvation. Chapter 5 of the *National Directory for Catechesis* describes liturgical catechesis for the sacraments and the liturgical year, as well as sacramentals, popular piety, and devotions.

Relationship Between Catechesis and Liturgy

Catechesis both precedes the Liturgy and flows from it. Liturgical catechesis helps people to fully, consciously, and actively participate in the Liturgy. It also helps them to reflect on the liturgical actions, to discern the implications of their own participation, and to respond by witness and service. Liturgical catechesis promotes a more informed knowledge and deeper understanding of the meaning of the Liturgy and sacraments.

Liturgical and Personal Prayer

Prayer nurtures our vital and personal relationship with the living and true God. Personal prayer is God's initiative, and the response to that gift is prompted by the grace of the Holy Spirit. Personal prayer and liturgical prayer are both part of the life of the Church. Because catechesis seeks to lead individuals and communities to deeper faith, catechesis for prayer emphasizes the primary aims of prayer—adoration, thanksgiving and praise, petition, and contrition—and includes various prayer forms: communal, private, traditional, or spontaneous; gestures, songs, meditation, and contemplation. Catechesis for prayer begins when children see and hear others praying and when they pray with others, especially in the family.

Catechesis for Sacraments in General

The liturgical life of the Church revolves around the seven sacraments, with central emphasis on the Eucharist. Fundamental principles apply to catechesis for each of the sacraments. Catechesis for a sacrament should

- Present a comprehensive and systematic formation in the faith, one that integrates knowledge of the faith with living the faith
- Center on initiation into the life of the Triune God, and present Christian life as a lifelong journey
- Be appropriate to the age level, maturity, circumstances, language, and ethnic background of those being catechized
- Be directed to all members of the Christian community, and be offered within and through the whole community of faith
- Involve parents in the formation of their children
- Be integrated into the total catechetical program
- Focus primarily on the symbols, rituals, and prayers contained in the rite for each sacrament
- Enable the believer to reflect on the meaning of the sacrament received by implementing a thorough experience of mystagogia following the celebration

Official catechetical norms, guidelines, and other essential tools for catechesis on the sacraments are found in the *General Instruction on the Roman Missal* and in each of the specific rites. Other resources to be consulted are *Rite of Christian Initiation of Adults, Guidelines for the Celebration of the Sacraments with Persons with Disabilities*, the *Directory for Masses with Children*, the *Directory for the Application of Principles and Norms on Ecumenism*, and the *Directory on Popular Piety and the Liturgy*. (See the resource list at the end of this publication.)

The baptismal catechumenate is the source of inspiration for all catechesis. The formation has four stages: pre-catechumenate, catechumenate, purification and enlightenment that prepares for the reception of the Sacraments of Initiation, and post-baptismal catechesis (mystagogy). This process is an inspiration for the lifelong formation of the whole community. Catechesis takes place within the community through instruction and the celebration of liturgical rites for the purpose of living as disciples of Christ.

The fourth period, mystagogy, in the broadest sense represents the Christian's lifelong formation in faith. Lifelong catechesis takes many forms, including participation in the Eucharist and study of the Liturgy, study of the Sacred Scripture and Catholic social teachings, reflection on life events in the light of faith, and opportunities for prayer, spiritual exercises, and acts of charity.

Catechesis for Particular Sacraments

Christian initiation is celebrated in Baptism, Confirmation, and Eucharist. Through these Sacraments of Initiation, believers are drawn into the communion of the Holy Trinity. They become partakers of God's own life, are incorporated into the Body of Christ, and are strengthened for discipleship by the Holy Spirit.

God intended that all people be saved by Christ's self-sacrificial love. For this reason, Christ founded his Church to continue his work of healing and salvation through the power of the Holy Spirit. Christ cured many who were sick, exorcized demons, and forgave sins. His healing ministry is carried on in the Church primarily through the Sacrament of Penance and Reconciliation and the Sacrament of the Anointing of the Sick.

The eternal plan of God the Father for the salvation of all people is further realized by Christ through the Holy Spirit, in the Church, in the Sacraments of Holy Orders and Matrimony. These Sacraments at the Service of Communion contribute to the life of the Church, the Body of Christ.

Chapter 5 of the *National Directory for Catechesis* lists specific catechetical guidelines proper to each sacrament.

The Sacred: Time (Liturgical Year) and Space (Art)

The Paschal Mystery, the mystery of salvation through Jesus Christ, lies at the heart of the liturgical year, a cycle of feasts and seasons. Throughout the year, the Church celebrates this Paschal Mystery every Sunday, the day of the Lord's Resurrection. The liturgical year unfolds in a way that corresponds to the major events in the history of salvation in Christ. The Christmas season celebrates the mystery of the Incarnation. The Easter season recalls the mystery of redemption. Each is preceded by a preparatory season: the Christmas season by Advent, and the Easter season by Lent.

The weeks of the year not part of either Advent and the Christmas season or Lent and the Easter season are designated as Ordinary Time. During this time, the Church celebrates different aspects of the fullness of the mystery of Christ from week to week.

In the course of the liturgical year, the Church also honors Mary, the Mother of God and Mother of the Church under many titles. The lives of apostles, martyrs, and saints are also commemorated. The unfolding of the liturgical year offers constant opportunities for catechesis.

Sacred art, architecture, and music also serve a catechetical purpose. Sacred art is essential to the Church at prayer because it expresses the divine presence. The church building is a sign and reminder of the immanence and transcendence of God. Sacred music gives glory and praise to God and forms an integral part of the Liturgy; especially for the parts of the Mass, sacred music also enriches the people's active participation in the Liturgy. It also has a catechetical purpose: to invite the people to give glory to God, foster the unity of their minds and hearts, and draw them closer to Christ.

Sacramentals and Popular Devotions

Sacramentals are instituted by the Church in order to sanctify the lives of the faithful. They can involve the blessing of certain ministries in the Church such as catechists or lectors, certain states of life such as members of consecrated life, and certain objects such as church buildings, holy water, rosaries, or ashes. Catechesis on sacramentals should describe their relationship to faith in Christ and their function in the Church and in the lives of individuals.

Especially in light of the cultural, ethnic, and religious diversity of the United States, popular piety is a vital element in Catholic life, expressed in a variety of ways. As a mode of inculturation of the faith that is deeply rooted in the cultures represented, popular piety and devotions provide opportunities to encounter Christ in the particular circumstances of ethnic, cultural, and religious customs. Catechesis must give careful attention to the role of popular piety in the lives of people, especially in the lives of new immigrants. Devotion to the Blessed Virgin Mary deserves special attention because it is such an important part of worship in the United States among many different cultures.

Care must be taken to ensure that popular devotions enrich the Church's sacramental life but do not replace it. All devotions should also lead the faithful to a deeper sense of their membership in the Church.

6

Catechesis for Life in Christ

Catechesis for life in Christ seeks to inspire
individuals and communities to allow life in Christ to
be the vital principle of all their activity.

The Christian moral life entails living the call to holiness through transformation in Christ. The discipleship to which Christ has called all believers demands love and self-surrender. Catechesis for life in Christ is a catechesis of the Holy Spirit, the interior guide; a catechesis of grace, the love of God; a catechesis of the Commandments, of the Beatitudes, of sin and forgiveness, of human virtues, and of the twofold commandment of charity. This catechesis always begins and ends in Christ. Chapter 6 of the *National Directory for Catechesis* describes the catechetical principles and guidelines needed for personal and social moral formation, as well as the witness that is to be given to the new life in Christ by individuals and by the community of faith.

The Dignity of the Human Person

All Christian moral life is rooted in the dignity derived from God's creation of us in his image and likeness. This divine image is present in every person. In Christ God reveals how human beings are to live. God created us with freedom: every person is a free and responsible agent with the right to exercise that human freedom, the capacity to choose good or evil. The more one chooses to do what is good, the more one becomes free. The choice to do evil is an abuse of freedom.

Secular culture often contradicts Christian values and threatens the dignity of every human being. Abortion and euthanasia directly attack innocent life; biological and technological developments can undermine human dignity. The treatment of people such as immigrants or undocumented persons, or of criminals and their victims, must be shaped by the awareness of the inherent dignity of every human person. In a culture in which freedom often means individual autonomy and personal choice, the individual person is pitted against society and social life, and even family life is emptied of its significance. Secularism, materialism, and ethical relativism erode moral reference points and thereby diminish people's ability to make moral decisions.

To address challenges to the dignity of the human person, catechesis on Christian morality must

- Uphold the right to life from conception to natural death
- Present the distinctly Christian understanding of human freedom
- Teach that freedom reaches its authentic goal in love of the weak and the defenseless and in defense of their rights
- Promote the public contribution of the Christian faith to public policy
- Encourage concern for the lives of the poor, the weak, the disabled, and the sick, as well as action on their behalf
- Help the faithful to make practical moral decisions in the light of the Gospel
- Encourage the faithful to understand that power, wealth, and productivity must be subordinate to and guided by higher moral values

Moral Formation in Christ

Christian moral formation involves conversion to Christ, including confession of faith, adherence to his person and teaching, and faithful discipleship. Divine grace transforms human nature so that a person can lead a morally good life. Virtue is the habit of tending toward the good and choosing the good in the concrete actions of a person's life. The theological virtues of faith, hope, and charity—the foundation of Christian moral living—transform the human capacity to do good into a participation in divine nature.

The formation of a moral conscience has to be rooted in the individual's relationship with Christ. Moral conscience is a judgment of reason whereby the human person recognizes the morality of a concrete act. It bears witness to the truth and judges particular choices, decisions, and actions to be either good or evil. Because the conscience can make erroneous judgments, people are responsible for ensuring that their consciences are well formed and that their actions reflect God's law, which is written on their hearts.

To communicate fundamental moral teachings, catechesis should restore a sense of the sacred and transcendent in life, to enable people to understand that God shares his own life with them and sustains them with his unfailing love. Catechesis helps people to form their consciences and make concrete moral judgments—to identify and recognize the effects of sin, an offense against God that turns the human heart away from his love. Sin wounds human nature and injures human solidarity.

Catechesis seeks to enable people to recognize and obey the divine law, based on universal truth and revealed by God, and to grow in virtue and commit themselves to a deep personal relationship with Christ.

The Human Community

The model for the human community is the Holy Trinity, the unity of Father, Son, and Holy Spirit. The very nature of the Trinity is communal and social. We who are made in God's image share this communal, social nature and are called to build relationships of love and justice. Christian morality has a distinctly social dimension that derives from the nature of the human person and the Church's social mission. Followers of Christ have the responsibility to apply Christian values to social systems, structures, and institutions in an effort to root out injustice. The Church's social teaching is a living tradition of thought and action, a framework that includes the totality of Christ's moral teachings and those proposed by the Church in his name.

The Church's emphasis on the social dimension of morality has led to the development of the concept of social sin, that is, personal sin expressed in the structures of society with social implications. Sinful structures contribute to social relationships that cause systematic denial or abuse of the rights of certain groups or individuals. Organized social injustice, institutionalized racism, systemic economic exploitation, and widespread destruction of the environment are examples of the social consequences of sin. Despite the difficulties in eradicating these evils, individuals are moral agents and need to work with others to change those structures and systems that cause evil.

Moral Formation in the Gospel Message

The Church has the responsibility to form its members in light of the Gospel and to teach them how to apply Christian moral principles to contemporary problems in specific and practical ways. The Ten Commandments (Decalogue) and the Beatitudes are the primary reference points for the application of Christian moral principles. The Decalogue expresses God's covenant with his people and is a privileged expression of the natural law that sums up love of God and neighbor. The Beatitudes teach the attributes and virtues to be cultivated in those who follow Jesus.

Other teachings of the Church that provide moral principles for Christian life are found in the Spiritual and Corporal Works of Mercy, the Theological Virtues and moral virtues, the seven capital sins, and the Precepts of the Church. Sacred Scripture and the lives of the saints provide concrete positive examples of Christian moral living. Those being catechized should not only know the Ten Commandments and the Beatitudes by heart but also understand how the teaching of the Beatitudes was already implicit in the Decalogue. In general, catechesis should present the teaching of the *Catechism of the Catholic Church* on the Decalogue in light of Christ's teaching in the Sermon on the Mount. Chapter 6 of the *National Directory for Catechesis* presents guidelines for each of the Commandments in order to assist the catechist in presenting the meaning of the Commandments and Beatitudes in a comprehensive and authentic manner.

7

Catechizing the People of God in Diverse Settings

The Church's catechesis presents the universal truth of
the Gospel to every stratum of human society, in a
wide variety of catechetical settings, in an effort to
transform society and renew the face of the earth. In this
catechesis, the Church recognizes and celebrates
diversity within the community of faith, affirms the
fundamental equality of every person, and acknowledges
the need for charity, mutual respect, and justice
among all groups in a pluralistic society in
ushering in the Kingdom of God.

Teaching was central to the ministry of Jesus. He was sent by the Father to proclaim the coming of the Kingdom of God and to draw humanity into communion with the life of the Holy Trinity. For two thousand years the Church has taken up Christ's command to go, make disciples, and teach. The Church is both the principal agent of catechesis and the primary recipient of catechesis. Every individual has the responsibility to grow in faith and to contribute to the faith of the other members of the Church. For this endeavor, the Church must take serious account of the circumstances and cultures in which the faithful live in order to present the meaning of the Gospel in an understandable way. Chapter 7 of the *National Directory for Catechesis* offers principles, guidelines, and criteria for presenting the Gospel to different groups in their diverse settings.

Catechesis According to Readiness and Age Levels

Growth in faith is related to human development and its stages.

Adult catechesis should be the foundation that gives coherence to catechesis for all ages, from children to the elderly. The goals of adult formation—conversion, participation in the Christian community, and discipleship—serve as the umbrella for all other forms of catechesis. The content of adult catechesis is directed toward discipleship developed through doctrine, celebration, moral formation, prayer, community participation, and missionary spirit. (A full treatment of the content of adult catechesis is found in *Our Hearts Were Burning Within Us*.) Methodology for adult catechesis varies, but this catechesis is always a basic, organic formation in the faith that includes a serious study of Christian doctrine integrated with formation in Christian living.

The *National Directory for Catechesis* offers specific guidelines for catechesis of other age levels.

The catechesis of *elderly* people is most effective within the context of a comprehensive program of pastoral care. Often, the elderly themselves are the most effective catechists for their peers and therefore need to be given the same opportunities for formation that are provided to all catechists.

Young adults should receive special consideration as they search for meaning in their lives, during a time in which they are often making important life decisions. As they face the challenges of many negative influences of society, they are vulnerable to feeling apathy, cynicism, and indifference to God and the Church. Catechesis for young adults should take place within the context of comprehensive pastoral care that addresses the questions they ask and recognizes the problems they face.

Significant physical and emotional changes characterize the period of *pre-adolescence and adolescence*. Just as with young adults, the most effective catechetical programs combine catechesis, community life, evangelization, justice and service, leadership development, pastoral care, prayer, and worship. Two areas of special concern are catechesis for the Sacrament of Confirmation and catechesis for Christian vocation.

The formation of *infants and children* begins in the home. Although it is generally informal, unstructured, and spontaneous, early formation is crucial to the child's development in faith. Structured catechesis begins in catechetical programs suited to the age, circumstances, and learning ability of children and is designed to reinforce the Christian values found in the family. The school and parish, through the witness of adults, provide an environment in which young people can grow in faith. At this age level, catechesis is gradual and systematic, integrating knowledge of the faith, liturgical life, moral formation, prayer, community life, and a missionary spirit.

Catechesis for Persons with Disabilities

Persons with disabilities are integral members of the Christian community and should be welcomed into ordinary catechetical programs as much as possible. Catechesis for some persons with disabilities, however, can require more personal attention or special access services (such as sign language interpretation) to meet specific needs. For those with developmental disabilities, involvement of families or other caretakers is essential because they are a resource for understanding the needs of the individual.

Catechesis in Special Situations

The community of the baptized comprises many different groups of believers, each of whom has the right to adequate catechesis. Special groups may include professional people, the marginalized, the socially and economically disadvantaged, college students, military personnel, unwed parents, married couples, homosexual persons, the divorced or widowed, and males or females. As much as possible, catechesis should be developed in consultation with those for whom it is intended so that it can better help them respond to God's uniquely personal love for each of them within the context of their special situation.

Catechesis in the Context of Ecumenical and Interreligious Dialogue

Catechesis helps to form a genuine ecumenical attitude in those being catechized. In order to engage in authentic ecumenical work, Catholics must know their own tradition well enough to be able to present the doctrine of the Church clearly and unambiguously, in a considerate manner that honestly presents the differences but avoids placing obstacles to dialogue. Catholics must likewise present the teachings of other churches and religions correctly and honestly, taking care not to misrepresent them. Catechesis must teach Catholics to respect the faith of others.

While ecumenical formation is necessary for all the Christian faithful, catechists in particular must have a firm grasp of basic Catholic principles of ecumenism. The *Directory for the Application of Principles and Norms on Ecumenism* is a resource for ecumenical formation of catechists. (See resource list for information about obtaining a copy.)

Special care should be given to catechesis in relation to Judaism, seeking to foster a correct and fundamental understanding of its history and traditions. Catechists must take care to affirm the value of the whole Bible and to appreciate the special meaning of the Old Testament for the Jewish people. Catechesis should teach both the independence and the interconnectedness of the Old and New Testament, emphasize the Jewishness of Jesus and his teachings, and show that Christians and Jews together consider the Ten Commandments to be a foundation of morality.

Catechesis in relation to other non-Christian religions has distinctive characteristics. Catholics need to be familiar with the history of Islam and its beliefs in order to work for mutual understanding. Catechists must be well informed not only about Islam but also about other non-Christian religions in order to promote respectful relationships with all peoples. Because the United States includes many new religious and spiritual movements, sects, and cults, catechesis in relation to New Age movements should accurately describe their tenets and carefully contrast them with Catholic beliefs and practices. The proliferation of these new movements reveals a hunger among many to find transcendent meaning in their lives. Christians need to reach out to others, offering the Gospel and the richness of our Christian spiritual tradition, which responds to the deepest longings of the human heart.

8

Those Who Catechize

Catechesis takes place in the many settings and
all levels that make up the Church: family, parish,
diocese, and nation. Catechists are called from a wide
variety of backgrounds and talents. These catechists and
these settings reflect life in the Holy Spirit. Nourished by
prayer, the celebration of the Eucharist, and the building of
community, they make catechesis ring true in the
hearts and minds of those to whom the catechist is sent.

Although all members of the community of believers in Jesus Christ participate in the Church's catechetical mission, Chapter 8 of the *National Directory
for Catechesis* focuses on the roles and responsibilities of those who are called
to more specific catechetical roles and provides principles, guidelines, and criteria for their formation as catechists.

Differing Roles of Those Who Catechize

Since the proclamation and transmission of the Gospel are central to the epis-
copal ministry, the *bishop* has primary responsibility for catechesis in the diocese. The bishop sees that the ministry throughout his diocese is supported by
competent personnel, effective means, and adequate financial resources. He
must also ensure that the catechetical materials used in the diocese transmit
the faith completely and authentically. The bishop might consider designating
a diocesan director and staff to aid him in this work.

Since *pastors* are the bishop's closest collaborators in ensuring that the goals
of the diocesan catechetical mission are achieved, they have a special responsibility. Pastors need to ensure that catechesis is provided for the parish celebration

of the sacraments and that the parish offers ongoing, age-appropriate catechetical formation.

Priests, parochial vicars, deacons, and *seminarians,* in collaboration with the pastor, have the responsibility of forming the Christian community and fostering the ministry of catechesis by providing catechists with training and support. The parish priest should play an active role in the catechetical program, being available to celebrate the sacraments with classes or groups and assisting catechists in carrying out their responsibilities. In order to enrich their ministry as catechists, priests and deacons need to give careful attention to their own catechetical formation. Seminarians need a clear understanding of the nature, goals, and methods of catechesis as well as the processes of human growth, development, and faith formation to prepare for their future ministry as parish catechetical leaders.

By virtue of their vocation, *those in consecrated life* catechize by the witness of their vocation and their apostolic work. Throughout the history of the Church, religious have committed themselves to catechetical ministry and are particularly suited to serve as parish or diocesan catechetical leaders.

The single most critical factor in an effective parish catechetical program is the leadership of a *professionally trained parish catechetical leader* who works under the direction of the pastor. Parishes must allocate essential resources to obtain a competent and able parish catechetical leader. *Coordinators of youth ministry* need theological formation as well as competence and experience in catechesis. Dioceses should provide training for youth ministers as well as catechists in general, including a certification program when possible.

While all members of academic communities have the opportunity to build up the Church on the university and college campus, the *campus minister* has a unique and important role. Campus ministry provides catechesis to students, faculty, and staff alike.

The Catholic school not only provides academic instruction of high quality but is also an effective means for Christian formation. Under the direction of the pastor or school board, the *principal* plays a critical role in meeting the catechetical objectives of the parish. In order for the Catholic school, as a center for evangelization, to have a distinctly Catholic identity and character, a catechetical program must be an essential part of the school. *Religion teachers* must have a thorough knowledge of the Christian message and the ability to communicate it. They also need to give personal witness to the truth of what they teach. The Catholic school is a particularly favorable setting for catechesis because it provides daily opportunities for proclaiming and living the gospel message.

Parents and guardians, as well as *families*, are the most influential agents of catechesis for their children. They catechize primarily by the witness of their Christian lives and by their love for the faith. Parents or guardians are catechists for their children precisely because they are parents or guardians, not because they have developed any specialized skills. When children are baptized, parents accept the responsibility to bring up their children in the practice of the faith. At the same time the Church promises to help parents foster their children's faith. Parish life with its celebration of the Liturgy, vibrancy of the community, adult catechesis, the parish school, and catechetical programs for children and preparation for sacraments is an aid to parents and guardians.

Preparation and Ongoing Formation of Catechists

In the Church's catechetical ministry, many catechists are volunteers who bring a wide variety of talents and abilities to the vocation of catechist. The call to be a catechist is not arbitrary but is instead a process of discernment involving the catechist, pastor, and parish catechetical leaders. When the pastor invites an individual to become a catechist, some form of commissioning ceremony should be held (preferably on Catechetical Sunday, typically held in September) to express the Church's call and the catechist's generous response. Those who have a specific ministry to catechize should strive to develop their human and spiritual qualities as well as their catechetical skills. The *National Directory for Catechesis* offers guidelines for catechetical formation, both in the initiatory stage and in the ongoing formation of the intellectual, spiritual, and apostolic life of catechists.

The formation of catechists takes place most effectively within the local parish. Parish-centered programs remind the catechists that their call comes from the Church, that they are sent by the Church, and that they hand on the faith of the Church. Parish-centered programs offer opportunities for the formation of a local community of prayer, mutual support, and learning.

Opportunities for catechist formation are also provided by the diocese. The development of comprehensive catechist certification programs, institutes, workshops, and seminars are within the purview of the diocese. Some dioceses work closely with Catholic colleges or universities to set up training and certification programs. Productive use of distance-learning models can be another means of assistance for dioceses and parishes.

9

Organizing Catechetical Ministry

The presentation of the Gospel requires the best efforts of
the Church at every level and the tireless dedication of
the entire community of the faithful. National, regional,
diocesan, and parish catechetical structures
embody Christ's apostolic commission—to go and
make disciples, baptize, and teach—through practical
forms, functions, organizations, policies, and procedures.
These are essential if the Church is to be
faithful to her mission in the world.

Within catechetical ministry is a diversity and complementarity of responsibilities, as well as the need for coordination of those involved in catechesis. Chapter 9 of the *National Directory for Catechesis* offers principles and guidelines for the development of a comprehensive pastoral plan at the parish, diocesan, and national level.

General Principles and Guidance

- Organization at the parish, diocesan, and national levels should be part of an overall pastoral plan that comes from the church's comprehensive mission.
- Organization for catechesis is person-centered, with particular support for the family as the basic community, and encourages participation of all the catechized in determining organizational structures.

- The goals of catechesis, accountability, and channels of communication should be clearly stated.
- Organizations should ensure equitable distribution of services, resources, and opportunities. Parishes in need should have opportunities equal to those of more affluent parishes.
- Essential aspects of catechetical organizational planning are analysis of the diocesan situation, assessment of needs and resources, identification and prioritization of goals and strategies, establishment of a realistic budget and overall working plan for the catechetical mission, and periodic review and evaluation.

Diocesan Structures

In the diocese, the referent point for the organization of catechetical pastoral care is the bishop and the diocese itself. The bishop has the final responsibility for a catechetical plan and its success. He may consult with a variety of bodies, such as various diocesan councils, in establishing and implementing a catechetical plan. The bishop relies on a diocesan catechetical director, through which he can direct and moderate the catechetical activities of the diocese. Since catechesis is an integral part of other diocesan offices, collaboration among the different agencies is imperative.

The Parish Community

The parish is the preeminent setting for the catechesis of adults, youth, and children. Like the diocese, every parish needs to develop a coherent catechetical plan. Sometimes this is done through a catechetical committee or commission that helps to plan, coordinate, and implement various catechetical activities within the parish. The members of the committee or commission should represent the diverse age, ethnic, social, and economic backgrounds present in the parish.

Some Pastoral Efforts

Comprehensive parish-based catechesis harmonizes all segments of the parish so as to allow a realistic opportunity to grow in understanding and practice of the Catholic faith. Careful consideration can also be given to the possibility of cooperating in *extra-parochial* or *inter-parochial efforts*. Smaller neighboring parishes might consider combining catechetical programs and personnel, especially if a single pastor is shared by two parishes.

Within the parish catechetical plan, priority should be given to *adult catechesis*, allocating funds for programs and for the personnel, time, and space needed for programs in adult faith formation. Other pastoral efforts in parishes can focus on *family-centered programs* that can help strengthen the bonds of the family, particularly interchurch families. Parents who choose to catechize their children at home are part of the parish's total catechetical effort. They need to be supported and guided in a curriculum approved by the diocesan bishop, need to be encouraged to fully participate in the life of the local parish, and need to attend appropriate training sessions provided by the parish or diocese.

All parishes provide *catechesis for children of all ages*, whether they attend Catholic or public schools or are home-schooled. Effective organization of parish catechetical programs for children should include enthusiastic evangelization and recruitment efforts to reach families whose children do not participate in parish activities.

Catholic schools, vital to the church's mission of evangelization and catechesis, are an integral part of the total parish catechetical plan. The Catholic school should strive to integrate the Catholic faith into every aspect of its life, seeking to relate all human culture to the Gospel so that the life of faith will illuminate all knowledge that is part of the school curriculum.

Youth catechesis is yet another aspect of the Church's catechetical mission. It is most effective when situated within a comprehensive program of youth ministry that includes social, liturgical, and catechetical components as well as opportunities for service.

The *baptismal catechumenate* is a vital component in the organization of catechesis in the parish and should be the cornerstone of the parish catechetical plan. The catechetical plan of the parish also needs to include a process of initiation for candidates for full communion who are already baptized. This process should respect the particular circumstances, experience, knowledge, and Christian practice of each individual.

Small Christian communities, found in many parishes, are important centers for the development of Christian virtues and human values. They often provide the faithful with an experience of a more intense community life. Since small Christian communities provide a natural setting for adult faith formation, the catechesis offered in these communities should be consistent with other elements of the parish catechetical plan.

While the parish remains the primary setting for catechesis, *other structures are beyond the boundaries of a single parish*. For example, some Catholic schools are regional or private schools not connected to a single parish. Other examples include catechetical programs for persons with disabilities, daycare and after-school programs, convalescent and nursing homes, residential facilities for persons with physical, mental, or emotional disabilities, and other organizations outside the parish but under church auspices—all of which should have a catechetical dimension.

Regional and National Associations

The formation of the faithful involved in a number of professional groups, movements, and associations that provide opportunities for religious devotion and apostolic service should always include catechesis. All of these organizations are to be integrated into the diocesan catechetical plan, in collaboration and communication with the diocesan bishop and local pastors. Dioceses also need to be aware of and to make use of information and resources provided by independent national organizations and associations.

The Service of the United States Conference of Catholic Bishops (USCCB) and of the Holy See

The USCCB has established a standing Committee on Catechesis within its permanent structure and has provided personnel and resources for its effective operation. The purpose of this committee is to serve the bishops in addressing the catechetical needs of the country as a whole.

The USCCB works closely with the Congregation for the Clergy, which assists the Roman Pontiff in the exercise of his ministry to proclaim and hand on the Gospel of Jesus Christ to the ends of the earth.

10

Resources for Catechesis

Catechetical aids that are faithful to God's Revelation of the truth in Jesus Christ and suited to the particular needs of those to be catechized can be very effective in the hands of skilled catechists. These materials should reflect fidelity to authentic doctrine with adaptation to specific circumstances.

No catechetical materials, resources, or tools—no matter how excellent—can replace the catechist. But sound catechetical resources in the hands of faithful and skilled catechists can be powerful instruments in proclaiming the Gospel and fostering growth in faith. Catechetical resources are many and varied: Sacred Scripture, the Church's official documents and catechisms, catechetical textbooks and other instructional materials, multimedia resources, and various means of telecommunications technology. Chapter 10 of the *National Directory for Catechesis* provides specific principles, guidelines, and criteria for developing, producing, selecting, evaluating, and using these materials.

Resources in General

The preeminent source for evangelization and catechesis is Sacred Scripture. Catechesis should make frequent, direct use of biblical texts and should present the Gospels in a way that elicits an encounter with Christ.

The *Catechism of the Catholic Church* is the authoritative contemporary expression of the living Tradition of the Church and a re-presentation of the deposit of faith in today's world. This basic resource for all catechetical activity provides a reliable guide for instruction and formation in Christian faith and life. One of the primary aims of the *Catechism of the Catholic Church* is to assist the bishops and the Christian people in the preparation of local catechisms. Local catechisms are invaluable because they take into account various situations ánd cultures, while preserving the unity of faith and catholic doctrine. A local catechism always requires the approval of the Holy See, which recognizes the catechism as a text of the universal Church that has been prepared for a specific culture and situation.

Catechetical Textbooks and Other Instructional Materials

In the United States, catechetical textbooks for children and youth are ordinarily part of an integrated series that has been prepared for a number of grade or age levels. Materials for adults often take the form of adult catechisms or resources for the baptismal catechumenate, for parish renewal, and for small Christian communities. Catechist and teacher manuals are essential components of a sound catechetical textbook series. Other instructional materials includes parent education material, resources for the baptismal catechumenate, and additional sacramental materials that enrich knowledge of the curriculum. Supplementary materials should be well integrated into a basic textbook series, in conformity with the *Catechism of the Catholic Church* when possible, and be artistically sensitive, technically up-to-date, theologically authentic, ecumenically accurate, and methodologically sound.

Communications Technology and Catechesis

Television has made a dominant impact on the education and formation of children. Consequently, the use of media is now essential in evangelization and catechesis. Contemporary communications media, however, do not merely transmit information; they generate visual, audible, emotional, and, in some cases, entirely virtual experiences for individuals and communities. Well-planned catechesis must employ these media so that the message of Jesus Christ can be effectively communicated in the real circumstances and culture of those who seek him.

Media take many forms, including print, audio-visual, and electronic materials. It is important that catechists receive training in the use of media, including the specific characteristics of different media, ways to distinguish between reality and virtual reality, ways to identify the primary and secondary messages communicated, and opportunities to become proficient in the use of the equipment. A parish or diocesan plan should include instruction on how to evaluate the media messages in light of the Gospel. An awareness of the techniques used by advertisers to influence and manipulate is critical, as is the ability to distinguish between the image presented and the reality or the distortion of reality that it represents. Viewers must understand the profit motives of commercial television and the Internet.

Preparation and Evaluation of Catechetical Materials

All catechetical textbooks and other materials are to be prepared according to the criteria and guidelines contained in the *National Directory for Catechesis*. General guides are the *Catechism of the Catholic Church* and the *General Directory for Catechesis*. In particular, authors, editors, and publishers should adhere to the guidelines for the preparation of catechetical resources in *Guidelines for Doctrinally Sound Catechetical Materials*. A further refinement of that document is found in the *Protocol for Assessing the Conformity of Catechetical Materials with the Catechism of the Catholic Church*. The fundamental criteria for guiding the development of catechetical materials derive from the principles of authenticity and completeness.

The preparation of catechetical materials should also be based on sound principles of catechetical methodology and take into account the cultural, racial, and ethnic diversity of those who use the materials.

The local bishop makes the determination about which catechetical materials may be used in a particular diocese. The bishop should establish a process for evaluating catechetical material, assessing both the doctrine presented and the methods used and taking into account the foundational documents, the diverse communities, and consideration of the overall diocesan catechetical plan. The bishop might call upon his diocesan catechetical staff to coordinate this evaluation process, inviting a representative group of pastors, principals, parish catechetical leaders, teachers, catechists, and parents to serve on a catechetical material selection and evaluation committee.

Conclusion

The *National Directory for Catechesis* provides the fundamental theological and pastoral principles drawn from the Church's teaching and offers guidelines for applying these principles within the catechetical mission of the Church in the United States. The *National Directory for Catechesis* was developed by the bishops of the United States to be a source of inspiration for a new evangelization and for a renewed catechesis in the dioceses and parishes of this country. This renewal should lead those who seek Christ to know him ever more deeply and to bear courageous witness to him in an increasingly secular world. It will only reach this goal insofar as it is a renewal in the Holy Spirit by the Holy Spirit.

May the Virgin Mary, whose intercession was once responsible for strengthening the faith of the first disciples, obtain for the Church in the United States the outpouring of the Holy Spirit, as she once did for the early Church. This gift will then make present the new evangelization and revitalized catechesis to which Christ's disciples of the new millennium will be his powerful witnesses.

Resources

Papal Documents

John Paul II, *On Catechesis in Our Time (Catechesi Tradendae)*. 1979. Washington, DC: USCCB.

Paul VI, *On Evangelization in the Modern World (Evangelii Nuntiandi)*. 1975. Washington, DC: USCCB.

Vatican Documents

Catechism of the Catholic Church, 2nd. ed. 2000. Washington, DC: USCCB–Libreria Editrice Vaticana.

Directory for the Application of Principles and Norms on Ecumenism. 1993. By the Pontifical Council for Promoting Christian Unity. Washington, DC: USCCB.

Directory for Masses with Children. 1973. By the Sacred Congregation for Divine Worship. In *The Liturgy Documents*, volume 1, 4th ed. (pp. 291-304). Chicago: Liturgy Training Publications, 2004.

Directory on Popular Piety and the Liturgy: Principles and Guidelines. 2002. By the Congregation for Divine Worship and the Discipline of the Sacraments. Available at http://www.vatican.va/roman_curia/congregations/ccdds/documents/rc_con_ccdds_doc_20020513_vers-direttorio_en.html

General Catechetical Directory. 1971. By the Sacred Congregation for the Clergy. Available at http://www.vatican.va/roman_curia/congregations/cclergy/documents/rc_con_cclergy_doc_11041971_gcat_en.html

General Directory for Catechesis (GDC). 1998. By the Congregation for the Clergy. Washington, DC: USCCB.

USCCB Documents

General Instruction of the Roman Missal (GIRM). 2001. By the International Commission on English in the Liturgy (ICEL) and the USCCB. Washington, DC: USCCB.

Guidelines for the Celebration of the Sacraments with Persons with Disabilities. 1995. By the USCCB. Washington, DC: USCCB.

National Directory for Catechesis (NDC). 2005. By the USCCB. Washington, DC: USCCB.

Our Hearts Were Burning Within Us: A Pastoral Plan for Adult Faith Formation in the United States. 1999. By the USCCB. Washington, DC: USCCB.

Rite of Christian Initiation of Adults (RCIA). 1988. By ICEL and the USCCB Bishops' Committee on the Liturgy. Washington, DC: USCCB.

Sharing the Light of Faith: National Catechetical Directory for Catholics of the United States. 1977. By the USCCB. Washington, DC: USCCB.